My Florida Alphabet

My Florida
Alphabet

Russell W. Johnson and Annie P. Johnson

Illustrations by John Hume

Pineapple Press, Inc.
Sarasota, Florida

We dedicate this book to our mothers, whose advice has always seemed to pay off:

"Clean your room!"
"Get a job!"
"Write a book!"

Inquiries should be addressed to:
Pineapple Press, Inc.
P.O. Box 3889
Sarasota, Florida 34230

www.pineapplepress.com

Library of Congress Cataloging-in-Publication Data

Johnson, Russell W., 1958–
My Florida alphabet / Russell W. Johnson and Annie P. Johnson. — 1st ed.
        p. cm.

ISBN 978-1-56164-392-9 (hb : alk. paper); ISBN 978-1-56164-729-3 (pbk : alk. paper)

        1. Florida—Juvenile literature. 2. English language—Alphabet—Juvenile literature. I. Johnson, Annie, 1942– II. Title.

F311.3.J64 2007
975.9—dc22

                                                        2006035339

First Edition
10 9 8 7 6 5 4 3 2 1

Printed in the United States

Introduction

My Florida Alphabet is not just another alphabet. Join Big Al, the tugboat, as he highlights various animals, characters, places, weather conditions, and such, that make the Sunshine State a great place to call home . . . or visit! So sing along, while performing the gestures for each letter.

Research continues to prove that adding movement, music, and rhythm while teaching a concept facilitates learning. We've seen it happen in our classroom, where we have used this approach for many years. Note that the song uses the *sound* of each letter as a preparation for reading. Teachers and parents will enjoy watching children learn their letter sounds as they see, hear, sing, and pantomime gestures for each letter.

The catchy "My Florida Alphabet" song, performed by elementary students, is easily learned, but not easily forgotten. **A CD with the song is included inside the back cover.**

Join Evy and Bel as they demonstrate each gesture through pictures. A written explanation of each gesture is included for clarification.

We've included reproducible "finger cards" for each letter at the back of the book. These can be used as flash cards or to create simple words through sound combinations (e.g., at, up, is, bag, etc.).

The variety of subjects used for the letters can also be a launching pad for studies in science and social studies.

So . . . hop aboard with Big Al as he navigates his 26 barges through Florida . . . and your child's imagination!

— Russ and Annie Johnson

My Florida Alphabet

Intro   I love my alphabet, I love my state.
       And I love learning . . . man, it's great!
       Put the three together, what do you get?
       You get an alphabet that just won't quit!

Aa   alligator
Bb   boat
Cc   conch shells (they don't float)
Dd   dolphin swimming oh so fast
Ee   Everglades, sea of grass   (PAUSE)

Ff   fishin' in the
Gg   Gulf
Hh   heron with a fish in its mouth
Ii   itch from mosquito bites
Jj   jellyfish (what a sight)

       (CHORUS)

Kk   Key deer (almost extinct)
Ll   lobster (tasty, I think)
Mm   manatee, gentle and slow
Nn   Naples (where the old folks go)   (PAUSE)

Oo   Osceola, Indian chief
Pp   Pennekamp, coral reef
Qq   quarter moon, time to sail
Rr   raccoon with a long, ringed tail

(CHORUS)

Ss	suntan on a winter's day
Tt	turtle floating on the bay
Uu	umbrella, always in reach
Vv	"varoom" at Daytona Beach	(PAUSE)

Ww	waterspout off the coast
Xx	extra juicy clams you can roast
Yy	yellowfly, "ouch, that stings!"
Zz	Zephyrhills, famous springs

CHORUS
Singin' my . . . Florida Alphabet
Stick around, you ain't heard nothin' yet
My . . . Florida Alphabet, sing along with me

7

Aa
alligator

Alligator — With arms straight and elbows locked, open wide and close.

Bb

boat

Boat — Mimic steering a boat (similar to car); twist left and right repeatedly.

Cc

conch shells

Conch shells — Place shell to ear and listen; then toss back in the ocean.

Dd

dolphin

Dolphin — Join hands, thumbs up, and dive, dive, dive.

Ee
Everglades

Everglades —With arms above head, sway left-right-left-right
(like grass in moving water).

Ff
fishin'

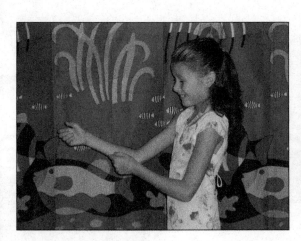 

Fishin' —Hold a fishing pole and reel in the big one!

Gg
Gulf

Gulf — Interlock fingers and create a fluid wave effect by up and down motion of hands and arms.

Hh

heron

Heron — One hand creates a beak while other hand (fish) is inserted into beak.

Ii

itch

Itch — Scratch those mosquito bites!

Jj

jellyfish

Jellyfish — Look surprised at seeing a jellyfish; step back and point towards the ground.

Kk

Key deer

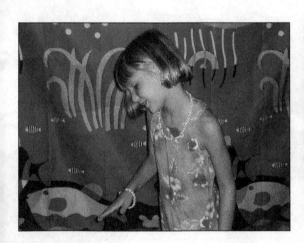 

Key deer —Kneel down on one knee and pet this miniature deer gently.

Ll

lobster

Lobster — With arms out to sides, elbows bent with hands upward, open and close claws.

Mm

manatee

Manatee — With palms together at waist level, the manatee swims upward in a fluid motion.

Nn

Naples

Naples — Role-play an older person. One hand holds cane, other holds aching back.

Oo

Osceola

Osceola —Stand tall and proud with folded arms and a serious look.

Pp

Pennekamp

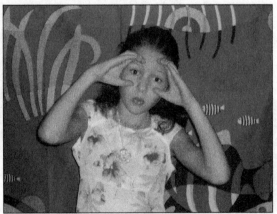

Pennekamp — Place a snorkeling mask on face; then look left and right for sea life.

Qq

quarter moon

Quarter moon —Reach up, grab sail rope, and pull down, hand over hand.

Rr

raccoon

Raccoon — Extend either arm to resemble a long tail; wave back and forth.

Ss

suntan

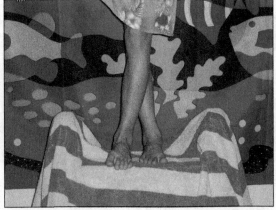

Suntan —While standing, cross legs, place hands behind head, and close eyes (vertical sunbathing!).

Tt

turtle

Turtle —With arms bent at elbows and hands near neck to resemble flippers, flip repeatedly.

Uu

umbrella

Umbrella — Hold umbrella pointing downward, then lift upward
and open it while looking up.

Vv

"varoom"

Varoom —With a look of excitement, point at a car and follow it with finger as it speeds by.

Ww

waterspout

Waterspout —Spiral pointer finger upward.

Xx

eXtra juicy clams

Extra juicy clams —Cup hands together (one on top, one on bottom) and open and close.

*NOTE: The X makes a "ks" sound. It is difficult to hear in the word "extra." We suggest you teach the "ks" sound in isolation.

Yy

yellowfly

Yellowfly — Hold arm out to side and *gently* slap that nasty yellowfly.

Zz

Zephyrhills

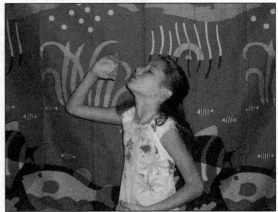

Zephyrhills —Hold bottled water in front of body; then unscrew the cap and drink.

Finger Cards

The following pages are "finger cards," one for each letter. You can reproduce them to use for further teaching of letter sounds.

Use them as flash cards. Show a card and ask, "What sound does it make? What letter is this? What are some words that start with this sound?"

You can use them to create simple words through sound combinations (e.g., at, up, is, bag, cat, lot, and, hat, dig, etc.).

Aa

Bb

Cc

Dd

Ee

Ff

Gg

Hh

Ii

Jj

Kk

Ll

Mm

Nn

Oo

Pp

Qq

Rr

S s

T t

U u

V v

W w

X x

Y y

Z z

Here are some other books from Pineapple Press that might interest you. For a complete catalog, write to Pineapple Press, P.O. Box 3889, Sarasota, Florida 34230-3889, or call (800) 746-3275. Or visit our website at www.pineapplepress.com.

My Florida Facts by Russell and Annie Johnson. Learn facts about Florida—from the state capital to the number of counties, from what states border Florida to how to make a Key lime pie. A kid-friendly book that makes learning fun by singing along with the "My Florida Facts" song, included on a CD. Ages 8–12.

Florida A to Z by Susan Jane Ryan. From alligator to Zephyrhills, you'll find Florida information packed into this alphabet—almost 200 facts about Florida personalities, history, geography, nature, and culture. For Florida's official gem, see M; for the saltwater mammal, see D. Ages 9–12.

Florida Lighthouses for Kids by Elinor DeWire. The history and lore of Florida's 33 lighthouses with fun facts and colorful illustrations. Learn about the people who designed and built them, meet some of the keepers, see how lighthouses operate, and discover their new roles as museums. Age 9 and up.

Lighthouses of the Carolinas for Kids by Terrance Zepke. A colorful and fun book filled with history and lore of the lighthouses guarding the Carolina coasts, from Currituck at the top to Haig Point at the bottom. Meet some of the keepers who braved storms and suffered loneliness. Learn how lighthouses operated in the early days and how they operate now. Age 9 and up.

Pirates of the Carolinas for Kids by Terrance Zepke. This book introduces nine of the most famous pirates to weigh anchor in the Carolinas, including Blackbeard, Anne Bonny, Stede Bonnet, and William Kidd. Age 9 and up.

Ghosts of the Carolinas for Kids by Terrance Zepke. Features 18 stories of spirits, monsters, and phantom pirates. Meet the Lizard Man, the Monkey Dog, the Gray Man, and the Little Red Man. Ages 8–12.

Iguana Invasion! Exotic Pets Gone Wild in Florida by Virginia Aronson and Allyn Szejko. Green iguanas, Burmese pythons, Nile monitor lizards, rhesus monkeys, and many more nonnative animals are rapidly increasing in population in subtropical Florida. This full-color book provides scientific information, exciting wildlife stories, and photos for the most common exotic animals on the loose, most of them offspring of abandoned pets. Age 12 and up.

The Gopher Tortoise by Ray and Patricia Ashton. Explains the critical role this tortoise and its burrow play in the upland ecosystem of Florida and the Southeast. Learn how scientists study this animal and try to protect it. Age 10 and up.

Those Amazing Animals series. Each book in this series includes 20 questions and answers about an animal, 20 photos, and 20 funny illustrations. Learn about alligators, bears, flamingos, turtles, vultures, and many more. Ages 5–9.

Drawing Florida Wildlife by Frank Lohan. Clear, easy method for learning to draw Florida's birds, reptiles, amphibians, and mammals, as well as the plants, trees, and landscapes that form their settings. Includes partially finished drawings for you to complete. Lists the tools and materials you will need. All ages.

Sinkholes by Sandra Friend. A clear and well-illustrated explanation of the phenomenon of sinkholes, which are born of the interaction between water and any rock that dissolves easily. Explains how a sinkhole becomes part of the environment, filling with water or becoming a deep, damp area that supports a new habitat. Reveals sinkholes from the oases of the Arabian Desert to the crystal-clear springs of Florida. Age 12 and up.